In a world of possible.......

dreamweaver

the   poems

Andrew Weaver   Sonja-Marié Peacock

.......Nothing is impossible

dreamweaver – the poems

AUTHORS ;

Sonja-Marié Peacock.
Born. Sasolburg South Africa, 1963
Scenic Artist, Artist, Poet and Creative Writer

Andrew John Weaver.
Born. Reading England, 1958
Fibreglass Design Engineer, Writer and Poet.

This book is of original poems from
"dreamweaver" the book.
By
Andrew Weaver and Sonja Peacock.

Dedicated to
All our friends and poets from around the world
and to all those residing at Poets Corner, CS.

Idea for cover picture from Peter Goodfellow

All Original Material Produced and Owned By ;
Andrew Weaver and Sonja Peacock.
Copyright : MP Dawn Publications - dreamweaver149@hotmail.co.uk

Published by Wilmots 2010 – vincent@wilmots.me.uk
ISBN 978-1-902778-06-8

- -
-

"dreamweaver" ….. the book.

"dreamweaver", A modern day love story of two strangers who meet on the internet. Though living thousands of miles in distance away from each other, they strike up a friendship. Unknown to them, 'dreamweaver' has taken an interest in their friendship. "dreamweaver", is the story of that friendship, taking us to different times and dimensions. Battling Knights, Wicked Witches, and Faeries are but a few things encountered on the dream path, with a sprinkling of real life, just for good measure.

Life's greatest gift

Poem and Picture by Sonja-Marié Peacock

Life's greatest gift to me...
is just to be..

In The Beginning

It was an accident.............No............ It really was!

I had really had enough of women on that singles site. Them all saying that ALL they wanted was Honesty and Loyalty, along with a dirty great long list of other attributes they want to see in their dream man. Then...... Just when you start with the first thing on their wish list, they suddenly and, without warning, find someone else they urgently need to talk to.

So.....There I was, moving the pointer thingy on the screen, to sign out for the last time. When it hit the poetry tab and stuck there!

I didn't even know I liked poetry before then, I thought it was like........ A sissy, girly thing........Y'know.

.... And to start with, it was hell!.......... I mean, nothing worked!

But, there was this woman on there, and I liked her writing, dunno why, just something in it, it was different, know what I mean?

So......I ended up staying awake all night, just to write her a little poem to put on the site, I hadn't even looked her profile up to see what she looked like, and .....I mean it took me all night to do it,... Right......And she lived on the other side of the world, for Gods sake!

It was after then, I started getting these dreams, really weird ones! Well, not so much dreams, as feelings and happenings,....... Experiences, Y'know.........One of those things, you can't quite put your finger on! But, you just KNOW it's there!

Then..........It was Amazing, I just started to write.........................Not all in perfect poetry.........Just what I saw.........

"dreamweaver"

We all dream,
you are there, you wander through them,
choose, one or two,
here and there,
a couple at a time,
as, and when, it pleases you to,
just taking them,
as you do.
With a touch, like a feather, so light,
sweetness of mind,
in thought, of a kind,
intangible colours, softly flowing,
of honest hue.
A magical aura, gently glowing,
with genuine affection,
true hope growing.
Cosseted, fondly nurtured,
supported,
coaxed and persuaded,
like a beautiful flower,
with wisdom watered,
all gathered, subtly altered,
cared for, sorted.
Then woven, with threads so mysterious,
included of all life's essence,
soft incandescence,
finally, making sure,
everything is golden and of benevolence.

Dragon

No mere mortal he!
With legs, neck gripped,
his master, on huge back did sit,
then,
harness pulled,
upward,
speedily onward, sky beckoned,
lightning flickered,
route to be taken,
through darkened, stormy weather,
by instinct reckoned.
Awesome power... Flapping, Beating,
causing,.... Draft for flight,
and long journey, into night,
with, Thoughts of two fates meeting.
Huge wings of bone and leather,
he, masters beast, loyal as ever,
Of a sudden, borne aloft!
Look up....
See underbelly, green, yellow, soft.
Huge talons, twin crystals clutched,
never before by mortals, seen nor touched.
Flaring nostrils.... Fiery breath,
lighting the way, by glowing coal red eye,
that does Intelligent strength imply
course charted, From this dimension to the next!
Always there, ready, for hour of need!
Kindly,
Vision of majesty,
DRAGON, Dear dreamweavers Steed!

While there is hope there is everything

You're out there somewhere,
You know?
I don't know where you are,
I don't know how I know.
But you'll love me,
You know?
So,
Now I'm on my own,
Maybe that's why I feel so alone.
But look,
I have faith,
You know?
Time or distance is nothing,
You're not far now,
You WILL find me,
Soon.
You know

A place called home

"Shosholoza Ku lezontaba Stimela siphum' eSouth Africa Wen' uyabaleka
Wen' uyabaleka Ku lezontaba Stimela siphum' eSouth Africa"

...your train song run your tracks straight into my heart embracing me in your coat of arms-
to become the perpetual pulse in my veins... like millions of drum beats heard over miles...
at the hoist of your flag and with nine million bicycles in Beijing, i feel you under my skin
my labola has already been paid by the white crashing waves on an endless shoreline...
Nkosi sikelel' iAfrika written in my heart and for when the tale of my land is told...
my soul stands proud and firm in patriotism like the feet of the mineworker in his gumboots
a place of freedom-where Table mountain stands proud and tall-i've explored and ran wild into
your mix of the Ndebele's colourful world with a blend of endless inter-racial faces in
street-markets interacting just like the beads in a zulu woman's artwork, always with a story to
tell...
of metropolitan's existence - busy, hustling and trading in need for daily survival...
of jazz coloured street musicians playing saxophone echoing your tune into my lungs
dressed in brightly red and white standing at the corner of cape ratanga junction,
of daytime safari expedition's escaping into a bushveld where lions roar and springbok leaps
and the big five walks hand in hand in peace-the pride and joy of Africa...
Your taste of boerewors ,braaivleis, biltong and rugby still lingering at the tip of my tongue...
I am as content with your soil between my bare feet like the click in the Khoisan's language...
your remote corners of cave paintings ,wire artworks,sarie marais,fynbos, kwaito and karoo
with your sunny sky on my face and your Indian ocean's wind in my hair, i've explored
a world where the millions of happy smiling faces of your different cultures like woven baskets
always reflected a welcome like gold and copper and diamonds and Nelson Mandela...
"I'm leaving on a jet plane..." just to return back to you once again... my home in Africa

Shosholoza is a traditional South African folk song meaning 'Go forward, make way for the next man'. Xhosa, Ndebele and Zulu are tribal groups. Labola is a traditional custom whereby the man pays the family of his fiance for her hand in marriage. "Nkosi Sikelel i Africa" is part of the joint national anthem of South Africa. Boerwars, Biltong, a sausage and cured meat. Braai, a barbecue. Big Five, the 5 most difficult animals in SA, to hunt. Lion, Elephant, Cape buffalo, Leopard, Rhino. Cape Retanga Junction is a theme park in Capetown.

Moroccan dreams 1

I Was taken to a place the other day,
Wild and rocky, but gentle in a way.

The sunrise,
Crystal clear,
In the distance, a forest,
A cow on the beach,
A donkey bellowing, the goats echoing,
A cock calling all to wake!

I sit on high,
And if I were handed a crown,
I could be lord of all this enchanted land,
But change nothing of it, or anything take.
Its magical properties, Clean air, sea and sand.

It's Rugged,
Beautiful in a simple way,
No complications here,
No rushing to make hay today,

Funny but,
I never asked its name, and I don't know the way,
But I know where it is,
And in a dream ....
I will visit again!

Moroccan dreams 2 ....(About a friend)

Land of sunshine, land of dope,

just have one of these and get some hope

C'mon.

Mix this green with some baccy from my tin,

Then relax,

and enter a world where future is the past and present too.

Where life is love and dark turns bright,

where all that is wrong will soon be right,

Cool....Outa sight!

Where sharp tongues are blunt, square corners are round,

A misty world where colour is sound.

So, just light a spliff and live anew,

In a gentle place,

Where everyone's a friend and you love them back too.

Battles past

Hey you with the wind in your hair.
Throw caution away,
Have not a care.
Face the wind,
You'll not now be bettered,
Gone are the chains that had you fettered.
So now you're free,
What will you do?
Though you'll never forget when you had to scream till blue.
Remember...
It gets better every day
You made yourself right,
You made them pay.
So now just chill,
Smile, bear no ill will
Everyone knows, you're no fool,
You showed them all,
The victory's yours, now seize the day.

Ode for the Ambassador Tank

I salute you!
my "hidden treasure" in the depth of your soul...
I had been the pirate on the ship-wrecked island of greed
land of the big yellow desert sun...
luring her prey...little to be freed
....my paintbrush my weapon
you have crept into my heart
and left your imprint over me

My fingers touched the texture of your soul
....you whispered softly....i listened carefully
...with paintbrush and airless
...my heart guided passionately
And that day....
that day they filled you up with blue-green ocean water...
i cried sacredly
...my treasure chest was inside of you...

the big yellow desert sun
reflects on your surface now
the green algae finding way over the once painted stone-faces
red-brown rust & corrosion
Mother Nature becomes the last artist
You tell your own story...
Atlantis...
city under the sea... in all its glory

....I say thank you
for my treasure
paradoxical to my intent....
you've changed my life
your blue green ocean water cleansed my soul
you've cut me loose of my burden with your knife
I leave you behind like my lover
on the ship wrecked island of greed

Giving Up, Giving In

That gum tastes 'orrible,
And this lozenge,
Supposed to be peppermint,
Ain't much fun.
My cigarettes taste somehow worse today,
I couldn't smoke another one.
I know, I already tried,
Coughed and heaved,
Then choked,
Sat down and sighed,
"It's Easy", I heard a voice shout,
Don't buy anymore,
And put that bloody thing out

Gaia

What a beautiful idea,
When you think,
It's really clear
Oceans, Rivers and Seas,
Land from mountains to leas.
From lichen to a tree,
From microbes, to you and me,
All parts of a wondrous machine!!

To run with the wind

My grandad once told me this

When you run with the wind, you cast off your fears,
Not duck and dive,
But take it all and hide your tears.
You'll see everything, you must be brave,
Run faster, but with care
Step on no-one on your way,
You'll find the love and gentleness you crave.
Be short on anger,
Don't wait to be praised,
Listen to all,
Take some as truth,
See your hopes and aspirations raised.
And when one day, the wind has died to a gentle breeze,
You're sitting by the fire with loved ones,
Living a life of ease,
A voice from the past tells you,
You chose the right path in life,
You did well!
Then......Your little one asks,
How do you do it? You know,

Run with the wind, please, please do tell...........

Left unanswered

You only went for a take away curry,
Though I was hungry,
I said not to hurry.
I remember,
It was pouring rain.
After that, I remember my tears,
The sting, the pain.
I cried the night through,
Again and again.
If you want,
You could come back and talk.
You could tell me what I did wrong,
We could go for a long walk.
You don't have to come here on your own,
Just call me,
We can talk on the phone,
And if you're in any doubt,
I promise,
Talk, we can work it out.
I just need to know why?
Why you thought it was alright to make me cry.
But I will come through, you see,
I'll try.
Hah!
Bet you've got a new life now, I'm sure!
But does your new partner feel really that secure?
Do they KNOW when you tell them,
Do they BELIEVE?
That you won't just one day, up and, LEAVE

A bottle of wine to share with myself

A bottle of wine to share with myself,
It's been there for ages now,
(You know the one),
Just sitting on that shelf.
I know you can't come back,
I WISH you could.
It's only been a week but, since you went,
I seem hellbent on destroying myself.
The children miss you too!
Since you fell asleep that day,
Ben keeps asking me if there is a way,
That you can come back.
He's too young, can't you see?
To understand, It's I now and not WE!
Sarah made you a flower yesterday,
I just couldn't see through my tears, no way!
I tried to smile and held her close,
I told her, she was the best in all the world,
That, she and Ben were the most,
But I can't make up for you not being here,
I can't be alone, can't you SEE?
I'm angry now, COME BACK,
I don't want I anymore, I need WE.......

Half past Octember

Tick....Tock,
What's with the clock?
Half past Octember?
Three minutes past Sunday?
Seventy nine forty five?
Something's wrong!
Am I alive?
Hey!
That's not my age!
Quick,
Turn the page.
Give me a drink,
No, a cigarette.
Funny thing,
I don't smoke,
I think!
Something's not right!
Is it me?
Or, just tonight?
The badgers' lost it's spots,
The leopard it's stripe.
This doesn't float my boat,
Or, light my pipe!
Are things really this bad?
Or, am I......
Going, ever so slightly,
But, entirely....
MAD?

The faerie & the voice

The pencil sketched faerie was sitting on a mushroom
with a book opened up in her lap on a white sketchpad
Inside a pencil sketched birdcage
Chained to the birdcage to her ankles
Birdcage door wide open
The keys to unlock the chains from her ankles
Laying in front on the pencil-sketched grass
on the outside of the birdcage
was a pencil sketched deeply rooted tree on each side of the birdcage
roots interlinking with each other underneath the birdcage
In one of the tree branches in the righthand corner
was a pencil-sketched man laying on his side resting on one arm
hand resting in his hair smiling and
looking at the faerie in the birdcage
the pencil sketched faerie was nor happy nor sad
she looked content
but she was chained to her ankles to the birdcage
The faerie cried but not in the
Pencil-sketched drawing
she cried and bled inwardly
not showing her true feelings
until the Voice spoke:
"Take the faerie out of the cage, you are the faerie"
The pencil-sketched faerie immediately unlocked
The chains around her ankles with the pencil sketched key
Laying on the grass
Took her pencil-sketched book of wisdom
And flew right out of the cage
Right onto the next sketch pad
Where she became a pencil sketched faerie
Arms spread wide open
Laughing happily
no more chains
no black and white pencil sketched birdcage
no deeply rooted trees
she was free
The faerie has changed her destiny

A faerie storie

O'er woodland fell,
Next to the enchant'd waterfall,
In the magick Faerie glade,
where tryst twixt Unicorn and Faerie,
forever and will ever be made,
Stood Faerie with tear streak'd face,
Holding the head of her beloved Unicorn,
By his halter of magick lace.
Sad evil had invaded this hallow'd ground,
Poor dear Unicorn and Faerie,
Had this evil, found.
For, a bad man some time, past back,
Learned of how a Unicorn tear could heal,
And even from death bring back.
In case anyone tried to steal his find,
Had Hurt, defenceless Unicorn,
Til he cried and cried,
Til there were no more tears,
Poor unicorn was dry,
Then Buried Poison'd thorn in his hide.
Poor Faerie knew, if she took it out,
The poison would spill,
Kill them both, without a doubt.
Of a sudden o'er all Faerie land grew a chill.
One last kiss Faerie gave dearest Unicorn,
Then pulled it out!
On the ground fell poison thorn.
But Faerie queen all this did see,
And With a mighty effort summoned,
All the thousands of Faeries she could see,
From near and far, throughout the land.
Raised to her feet, and with all the magick, at her command,

Changed all that was done by that wicked mans hand.
Commanded peace and happiness be once more,
Throughout all of faerie land!..........
Now go to the Enchant'd Waterfall and see,
Reflection of Unicorn and Faerie,
In each others arms, and by Queen, commanded
This is the way,
It will always, and forever be.

~ ~ ~ ~ ~

The storie of Faerie Glade

The battle was almost done,
Evil Wizards and Goblins, had almost won.
Magick 'gainst Magick, Faeries had lost the day,
Wizards lightning, lighted Goblins ghoulish way,
And, all over the land, strewn,
Were Faerie Dead.
Unicorns, by Evil Goblins,
To, their final resting place, led.
All was chaos in Faerie land,
All done by Evil Magick'd hand.
Then, all that were left,
Were Faeries but ten, and Unicorns three,
All braced against Magick life giving Tree.
And, as they with Magick fought,
Many a thunderbolt, did strike poor Faerie,
Life taken, returned by tree, instantly.
So in this way, Unicorn and Faerie, did it protect
Then roots did sprout from ground,
Groped Wizard and Goblin, strangled, necked.
Then weaved a necklace round and round,

Til a way into Faerie by thunderbolt, could not be found,
Where Faerie found comfort in exhausted sleep,
And Unicorns, all night did weep,
Into hats that Faeries had made!............
When they finally woke, they found,
All over Faerie Land,
Evil Goblins and Wizards,
Lay'd by tree root, kill'd and bound,
Then hats of Unicorns tears they took,
To where dead Faeries lay'd,
With tears then, from the dead, living made.
And,
Finally, when all Evil was banish'd and staid,
Faeries and Unicorns, in thanks, to Tree,
Fashion'd and Magicked....Faerie Glade.

~ ~ ~ ~ ~

Nightmare on Church Street

It was only just last week,
We were sat in the pub,
She said she was miserable,
I said I was bored, we agreed,
we needed something different,
we were in a rut, we both needed a "Tweak".
THEN.............
I swear I don't know how, but here I am,
Perhaps I got too drunk, a bit too tight,
But there she is,
Scowling mother in law to be on my left,
My best mate stood there, just grinning,
On my right.

Marry in haste,
Repent at leisure,
I paid the vicar,
He smiled and said, "My pleasure",
It's my marriage day,
I should be afraid,
Because before long, she'll be,
Her indoors that must be obeyed.
They all wave us off,
We drive up the road,
Her, my princess,
Me, her ex toad,
"And Friday night out with your mates",
It won't stay good for long,
"And that oily motorbike, that'll just have to go",
Because as she keeps telling me, for many reasons,
She's right and I'm wrong, you know?
THEN...........
After a while, and all the insults I'll have carried,
It'll be, "You're no good now! You've changed!",
And then she'll say, as if it's all my fault,
"You're just not the man I married!"
THEN...........
I woke with a start,
Sweat on my brow,
It's not next week, I was dreaming,
Thank God, I'm still single,
It's still now!

Later, we were in the village walking.

She said, "Let's go to the pub, it's open, I heard the church bell",
I need a drink,"
I said, "Why not",
Then all of a sudden.......
I really, REALLY, didn't feel very well.

~ ~ ~ ~ ~.

Sherlock's Opium Dream (Part 1)

The darkened marsh,
Mist shrouded moon,
"It stalkes here, Watson",
"Does it?",
"By God, by Jove, by,...
What Holmes, I havn't a clue!"
"Why, DEATH Watson,
By hound or headless ghoul,
Wait and watch,
Pandemonium, the night will soon here Rule!"
"SHHHH! Quick hide, Look yonder",
"Holmes....... that's STUNNING,
A headless horse,
With a legless rider,
But why are they out at this time of night running?

to be continued.................

~ ~ ~ ~ ~

Young man, old soldier

I was a soldier.
I am that man,
Now just as then,
Getting by, the best I can.
From freezing, filthy bomb holes,
Lice ridden bodies,
To Christmas at home, by the fire,
Hot chestnuts and toddies.
Thinking.
It was insanity, When we fought
or was it fun?
Couldn't work it out then,
Now I'm out though, best I ought.
Screaming and shouting,
A hilarious joke, screeching laugh?
Or the sound of choking pain,
Bullets, bombs and rockets,
A seething, killing rain.
Then silence,
The battle was done,
Sergeant Major stood beside me and said,
"You got through it, you're alive,
good on yer kid, well done son".
His arm round my shoulder,
Me, weary thinking of the battle past.
"Go on son", He said,
"Find something small to take home"
"Be the first, you won't be the last".
Then it was all over.
I was sent home,
My country doesn't need me now,
After what me and "The Lads" have done.
Because we were ordered to kill and maim,
Should we hang our heads in shame?
Or should we stand proud?
Should we shout out loud, "We fought for you",

Or, did we do it for ourselves?
Should we say,
"It was all for your sake, in your name"!
How can we be easy on ourselves?...........
And when the next time comes,
When, yet again we must go to war,
Shall we ignore the rallying call?
Not on your life, I'm sure.
We'll be there when needed,
ONE AND ALL!

~ ~ ~ ~ ~

Just a day

Night ends with a chill,
Dew forms on the grass,
Mist thins and rises,
As the sun comes up in the east.
Moon sets.
Clouds travel the sky,
Sun goes down in the west.
Moon rising,
Just a day in the land where I live.

~ ~ ~ ~ ~

With freedom in mind

Grass high,
Running through it,
Wind in my hair,
Blowing through it.
Bars will hold me never,
Because in my mind,
My freedom is forever.

~ ~ ~ ~ ~

First rule of holes

I'm getting too old,
Smoke too many cigarettes,
Sometimes I drink.
A disaster, looking for a place to happen,
So I'm told.
Now I'm in a REAL HOLE, I think.
Forgot the golden rule see,
"When in one, don't dig"!

~ ~ ~ ~ ~

Sherlock's Opium Dream (Part 2)

...Off then, they rush in hot pursuit,
One with a bowler and three piece suit,
With the other a deerstalker bobbing,
Followed unseen, by a large white rabbit, ears flopping
Now three o're mist shrouded marsh are hopping.
Then....a drooling, ghostly hound,
Stalking silently, feet not touching ground,
Weighing at least two hundred pound,
Double rowed compliment of teeth like razors,
And red glowing eyes,
piercing the dark like lasers!
So, as our friends, through the dank marsh pick,
Hell Hound closer with every step,
Are they courting peril dire.........
....Or, has Holmes, up his sleeve,....
...A trick?........

to be continued.....

~ ~ ~ ~ ~

Witches brew (No. 2)

Hubble bubble, toils and troubles
See the pot my children,
How all within it,
Writhes and bubbles.

Tail of dog and eye of newt,
Paw of cat and tongue of mute,
Hair of love and one of spurned,
Three paces left then half right turn.

Leg of frog and left hand glove,
Wart of nose and beak of dove,
Tail of lizard and leaf of tea,
hair of hog and flea from flea.

Root of mandrake with skunk muste,
Spot from toadstool with fairy dust,
Dragon scorched earth with wiggly worm,
Three paces to the right then half left turn.

Wing of fly and sting of gnat,
Screech of owl and toe of bat,
Twig of new broom, that sweeps the room,
Stir all by starlight and beam of moon.

And when you want a new lover to come,
Look right, then left, then drink,
But, mark my words and heed them well,
Unless you want an ugly one,
Be within good sound of a bumble bee hum....

~ ~ ~ ~ ~

Lottery

Another day on the street, sat rattling my tin,
If I make enough money today,
I won't sleep out tonight, I'll sleep in
I keep trying to be the lucky one,
Will my numbers come up today?
Will I have won?
I have my doubts, but weekly I pay my coin in,
Surely the game is rigged, I think,
But know, if I don't bet...... I can't win!

~ ~ ~ ~ ~

Seamless

Like in a mirror,
We feel each other,
Asking nothing of one another.
When we look in each others eyes,
We're lost in something,
No words can describe.
Worlds, passing by in ignorant blissfulness,
There's just us,
No joins.....
...Forever...
..Seamless.

~ ~ ~ ~ ~

When I'm happy I whistle

When I'm happy, I whistle.
I smoke too much.
I'm getting old you think,
I work really hard,
So I blow off steam.
You just don't know,
How much I drink.
But...I'm a well oiled machine,
Don't clank or grind.
I'm the type,
To pull you out of anything,
If you're in a bind.
To be younger though...
...What wouldn't I give,
For my younger days,.....
When people thought,
I really I was...
A MAGNIFICENT Locomotive.

~ ~ ~ ~ ~

Sherlock's Opium dream (Part 3)

So.....
With a big white rabbit in tow,
Followed by hell hound, with ruby red eyes,
And teeth that flash,
Closing on their quarry, in headlong dash,
Glanc'd in a pool momentarily,
And with a splash,
Skidded to a halt,
On slimey ground, not quite sedimentary,
This magnificent clue Holmes had spotted,
Was important to him, like.... Elementary,
Razor sharp mind, churning, thinking,
While Watson stopped, already sinking.
Watson then with feelings mix'd,
Looked first at Holmes studying rabbit,
Then at drooling hound transfix'd.
What then of these three's fate?
With Watson sinking in foul smelling mud,
Holmes in blissful ignorance, feeling good,
Eyes watching hound Circling,
In close adjacent neighbourhood,
Drooling, with stench of hells gate.
.....If we want to know that my friends,
We'll just have to wait.

to be continued................

~ ~ ~ ~ ~

Because of your hurtful words...

I have bled in my soul
I have been so afraid to live
I have built high walls around myself
I knew the true meaning of the word fear
I could never know what it was to love again
I knew the real meaning of low-self-esteem
I had been a prisoner trapped in the past
I didn't wanted to be close to anybody
I had been confined to......... solitude
I had stopped....... communicating
I have kept the words inside........
I fear........ when you were near
I never....... shared my secrets
I knew the word rejection......
I have crumbled silently.....
I was so scared to trust.....
I have dreamt alone........
I couldn't open up.......
I never spoke...........
I have died..........
.......alive.......

~ ~ ~ ~ ~

About this poem:
The emphasis of the poem is more focused on the symbolic value & the visual shape of the words stacked together in the shape of a coffin : bury the past. The dark background, shape and dying words are all for visual impact...
I posted this poem after I re-read Shortstack15's poem this morning. The poem is about abuse towards a child – Sonja.

The best day in a child's life

I sat down beside him.

"I like cheese on toast, wiv peanut butter on top, and jam,
But...Sardines and tomatoes... That's my fav'rit",
Pulling a face now, Shaking his head,
"Don't like ham".

I smiled.

A four year old boy,
sat in a rubbish strewn yard, rats running around,
Playing with an old wooden toy.
He had dirt engrained hands and face,
Short trousers, scuffed and bleeding knees.
"I falled over, it's only a scratch",
I dabbed at them with my handkerchief.
Tough little blighter,
Knew better than to ask for anything at all with a "Please",

"You're a copper aint'cha...?"
"I can tell.... Mom'll be back soon. She'll give you 'ell".
No I thought, she won't,
She's gone to prison for a long time...Sat in a cell.

I took a deep breath.

"Come with me", I said,
"I'll take you away from here,
I know where you can get,
The greatest sardines and tomatoes you ever saw,
On best bread".
His face lit up.

Not looking back, we picked our way to the broken down gate.
I held his hand tight, to the waiting car I led,
Praying that one day, the worst of all this, he'd forget.

Act of the soul

We swim in the ocean of our own words,
With no composed lyric,
No painted picture,
No eloquent display,
No dramatic visualization,
No theatrical play.
No vivid imagination
No rhyme nor rhythm
No recognition nor sympathy seeked!

We listen to the written language of the Creator in our soul,
To become aware of acceptance,
We linger too long in the company of silence.
To reach this moment in time,
We walk a mile in the footsteps of darkness of the ones before us,
To reach the lighthouse within us.
We dwell in our analytical psyche,
To reach the sense of our existence.
We heal through the pain & blood of our own words,
To become healed.
We live & experience two sides of the same coin,
To heal the ones behind us.

Poetry is an act of the soul,
That sets us free………

A poem is born

Hold your pen loosely...Relax,
First, there's a Sense of......Something,
A slight tingling of the fingers,
In your head you start to feel,
Excited in a way,
An itch you can't scratch.
Almost as if they had always known,
Hand and pen to paper are drawn,
Then, like magic, words appear,
They seem to take on a life of their own.
Eerily you begin to "feel",
Life, through others' eyes,
You..."See"...What they think,
There is no veil of disguise.
All seems a senseless jumble,
Let it happen, doesn't matter,
All of a sudden ideas in mind clatter,
They sort themselves,
Then take form,
From which you choose what pleases you,
And....A poem is born.

~ ~ ~ ~

Under my skin

This poetry thing,
'S got under my skin.
These days I've less of a will,
And more of a chill,
Not as in Spooky, or BBBrrrrr,
But, like in relaxed.
It's easy man, just sit,
Let brain cogs WHirrrrr,
Wow.....See?
....Hours....Elapsed.

Friends

We're friends, you and me,
We see in each other, what others can't see,
I help you and you help me,
Through life's troubles equally,
So here's to us both, good friends we'll always be.

The end of a poets day, (For everyone here)

Well, that's it then!
The end of my day,
Got some ideas for tomorrow,
But, that's a whole sleep away.
I'm sleepy and tired,
All poeted out with not much more to say.
So thank you one and all,
I hope I have pleased some of you,
Be you, handsome, sweet and short,
Or beautiful and tall.
Whether you're here or there, doesn't matter
Because all around the globe, in poetry, we natter,
So May your God go with you,
And bless you one and all...!

Sherlock's opium dream (Part 4)

....Hound leapt with eyes flashing,
Watson ducked, heard teeth gnashing,
Then hell dog, Whoosh, his head passed,
It landed, turned, ready to charge,
When, of a sudden,
Large white rabbit, a spell did cast.
One of Holmes' dreams?
Had Holmes had some opium?
Is that why this pandemonium?
Then, still in confused thinking,
There they all were, in a big manor house,
In dinner jackets, smoking and drinking,
Then, Awful scream rents the air,
Twas a good job Holmes was there,
Sure there was something to be found,
He was up like a shot, faster than sound,
"MURDER", came another scream,
Surely,.... thought Watson....
....I'm stuck in some awful dream!...

to be continued.............

~ ~ ~ ~ ~

My key to me

Do you want me?
Can you say true?
If I give you the key to me,
Would you?
Would you KNOW what to do?
You could love me,
Or hurt me,
You could imprison me,
Or set me free,
Would you?
You can do anything with it,
It's the key to me.
It holds so much power!
You could make my world with a smile,
You could mortally wound me with a glower,
You can be gentle with me,
You can be rough,
so you see, this is my key,
I feel so helpless and weak,
I love you,
I have no choice,
in you I trust,
Here, take it, my key to me.

~ ~ ~ ~ ~

Love, our first time

We feel one another, with each others eyes,
A trembling....A pleasure begins,
We can't hide nor disguise,

Even breath, becomes ragged and fast,
Excitedly, tongues probe,
Exploring fingertips, gently caress,
Building slowly to ecstasy at last.

Then, desperation, anticipation,
Breath in short gasps,
Gripping now, locked in embrace,
Gasps become breathless,
With inevitable pace.

We're both wandering,.....
...Lost now....
In the same indescribable place,
Feeling, seeming on the brink of an abyss...
...Forever,

Then Quickly....Oh so beautifully...
...Our moment comes...
....For us both...
.....Together.

~ ~ ~ ~ ~

Solitary confinement of loneliness

The rebellious war against you antagonistically pitch black,

unscrupulously radiating the vortex force inside, bigger than myself.

So many a time my complexed-unwanted-overpowering obsession,

a solitary prison cell of my own creation - the size of myself -

single bar sunlight-overwhelming dark- i needed you most,

choosing your most delicate darkest corner of self-pity despite...

Subconsciously - a Buddhist monk's sanctuary of no spoken words

no choice left but to confront the inner tormentor of pain,

gladiator and full on face-to-face with my personal devil....

Finally surrendering traitorously yet immensely brave,

to found the answer hidden away like a treasure -ah a blindfolded fool!

To become aware of your immense internal power with grace

with the leftovers of my own personal peacock pride...

You became my stepping stone along my cobblestone path

guiding me on the biggest journey of my lifetime... the journey within.

So sad only later....many many many scarlet blood shed-tears later...

My disguised enemy became my best friend

...I take your hand......

Written at a time in my life when I felt extremely lonely...the feeling of finally accepting it was one of the greatest and most overwhelming feelings I've ever experienced.. And very ironically the moment I started accepting it-my outside world changed...because my inside world has changed... Sonja.

Love, in desperation

What do you mean, what is love anyway?
You're hurting me, please don't do that anymore.
I'll do anything you say.
I'll beg, I'll PLEAD,
Please, just don't walk out that door.
I was wrong, I admit it, I didn't know,
I won't do anymore wrong,
Please don't go.
I can be better than him
We've been together too long.
He JUST doesn't know what you NEED,
OK, So you've made up your mind,
You're leaving,
You never used to be this hard, you were kind,
I can't lose you, It's like you dying, You leaving,
Please don't leave me alone,
I can't do grieving

~ ~ ~ ~ ~

Because you can

So, what's it like,
To be soooh bad... you're good,
Soooh cool....You're hot,
Always seen at the best places,
Out of town when you're not,
To have a reeel tan,
Not one from booth or spray,
To always be seen with a girl on each arm,
Like you do...It's your way. Because you can,
I was like you once,
But hey,
Now... I'm a really happy man !

Sherlock's opium dream (Part 5)

....

...On instruction, Watson had gathered all,

....A nun in a habit,

In a dinner jacket, the large white rabbit,

Butler, stood holding handtowel,

Holmes, upstairs, sifting evidence of murder,

By hand, most foul.

About the place the air had settled,

Now one of gloom!

Then...A faint sniffling, not heard,

From the front door!

Many a scratch twixt dog a flea,

Had brought it here, via the biggest tree,

Arbiter of mischief and doom!

Hound from Hell, all the way here,

Had tracked them, for sure,

This multi faceted game, my friends,...

Is on, Again...Once more.......

to be discontinued...........

~ ~ ~ ~ ~

Murtaya

Yesterday, I said goodbye to my love,
We had spent three months together,
We were like hand and glove.
And as that plane went,
I felt sorry, I nearly wept.
Sometimes we had fought,
She bit, I shouted,
But always in the end, it came to nought.
She's gone to another place now,
But, I'll see her again one day, I vow.
She's gone with someone I used to call "Sir",
So, good luck and God speed,
To all, who may drive her!

~ ~ ~ ~ ~

About this poem :
About a prototype car that I built, it's racing round Canada as we speak. It was
a long, bitter sweet affair from beginning to end........

The oily rag

OO do you want?
Right....look,...Go down there,
Turn left at the font.
You CAN'T miss 'im.
Filthy, dirty, oil soaked overalls,
Greasey rag in one 'and, spanner in the other.
E'll be up a ladder,
Round 'is waist 'e ties a sack,
Look.... If 'e aint up or down...
'e'll be round the back.....
....Or underneath.
Are you stupid?
Listen,
You CAN'T miss 'im look..
Due to an accident,
'E's got a wooden leg an lost all 'is teef.
'e's four foot nine and fat and jolly,
stinks of swett.....
Yesterdays curry...wot 'e ett.
.........And....'e's only got one ear.
Anyway what do you want 'im for?
You ain't takin' 'im anywhere,
'E's my genius....'E's my Chief Engineer.

~ ~ ~ ~ ~

An ocean away

We're not worlds apart,
Just an ocean away,
I love you,
I'm coming,
Can't live without you, No way,
Our time is now,
Our day is today,
See you soon, my darling,
I'm on my way!

~ ~ ~ ~ ~

Life's house

Foundation first, this is a must!
Honest and solid,
To build some trust,
Then, in time
Walls, windows, doors and floors,
For your life,
Where you will always be together,
As husband and wife.
Finally, a roof to keep you dry,
You now have a house,
Where life can be lived, with no deception or lie.

~ ~ ~ ~ ~

Bridges

..You're looking across and see two sticks,
So, you put two as well,
Then, another two contriwise,
It's rocky first, but settles down,
Carry on building,
'Til from side to side,
The gap gets so small, it's not wide,
Then reach...Take the others' hand,
Hold on gently, balance to provide,
You're friends now,
All that way....From land to land

~ ~ ~ ~ ~

Wish for an umbrella

I saw her in the rearview mirror of my car,
as I drove past.
Walking along the highway,
bright yellow sunny day,
nowhere to go....

No shoes, dirty hair, torn dress, alcohol smell that overwhelms the car
skin that has been exposed to the yellow sun for too long...
One plastic bag containing all her worldly belongings
She didn't speak much and I decided not to ask much,
as she was sitting in the car seat next to me....

Deep, contemplating the thought
of making the wish of someone else's come true for one day.
As we entered the first town, I asks her if she is hungry
Yes... and can I please buy her some shoes too?
With the food stucked in her plastic bag.

We headed for the retail outlet selling clothes,
everything she wants today-she will get today...
ready to pay for the shoes, the toothpaste...
She notices the umbrellas displayed at the end of the till
can I please buy her an umbrella...just for in case it rains...?

Later that same day,
hours after I dropped her off...
I saw her laying on the green grass next to the railway track,
on her back, legs stretched wide open into the sky...
Admiring her new shoes.

Bright sunny day,
-rain nowhere in sight...
One, open colourful umbrella next to her
-just for in case it rains...?
Nowhere to go..

Life's dream

The stream of life past us flows,
where it goes, no-one knows.
the water is deep, the current fast,
And what was our future is soon the past.
The tree is high, the roots run deep.
It's branches spread wide, safe us to keep,
Leaves are our shelter, and warmth at no cost,
With buds that are our babies,
And Twigs our young, to replace,
Generations lost.

And so life's dream...
Twixt tree and stream,
One to watch and one to wait,
While those that have past,
Speak as guardians of the gate.
Always follow what's inside,
Forget the money,
Or what's gain'd in import,
Is lost to fate,
For sometimes with something that pays less,
You'll gain more reward, than you can guess.
A good way to start!
Only you know what's inside you,
What's inside your heart,
And you will soon find,
When with another of your kind,
Cool realisation, That bodies age, and looks fade,
But Never a Clever or Beautiful Mind.
So to your own self be true,
Feel deep inside,
Converse with your heart,
You'll know what to do!

Two sides of a coin...

After every tear in my life
-I found a reason to smile again
After every sadness in my life
-I found moments of joy again
After every hurtful word in my life
-I found someone to compliment me again
After every painful experience in my life
-I found a reason to enjoy life again
After every time I fell in my life
-I found someone to pick me up again
After every time I felt uninspired in my life
-I found someone to inspire me again
After every setback in my life
-I found a reason to live again
After every problem in my life
-I found a solution to better myself again
After every lowest point in my life
-I found a peak point again
After every quitting my dream in my life
-I found a reason to follow my dream again
After years in my life
-I found there was two sides of a coin....

Our book

You're the first page, I'm the last,
For All of our life story, I expect.
Everything in between, present and past,
All bound in a cover of love and respect.

~ ~ ~ ~ ~

Two sides of the same coin

You're one side, I'm the other,
Two sides of the same coin,
We're joined together.
Were we minted or smelted?
No, married, ...Then melted,
We had our fun,
Over time became one.
Then there's our third side,
Our arbitration place,
Where we can bury our pride,
Without losing face.
One thing is for sure,
We're certainly hearted,
Love one another,
And can never, ever be parted.

Homeless

Don't know what to do,
Sat here cross legged,
If I could think straight,
I might have a clue.
Barred window behind me,
In front, a door,
Walls to each side.
Then a clang! Policeman appears,
"Good Morning", friendliness implied,
Puts cup of tea on the floor,
He'll kick me out now,
Could do with more sleep,
Never mind, it was so much better,
Than another cold night,
Alone on the street!

~ ~ ~ ~ ~

About this poem:
We hope that everyone that reads this has a roof over their head tonight,
wherever they are. If you havn't, our thoughts are with you. xxx

That's Me

My feet are lovely,
My legs, perfectly formed,
Further up, I'm flat as can be,
See what I mean.... Just.....Feeeel me,
I have so many friends that gather round me,
Who's doing what with who, news, story or fable,
I've a steady disposition,
How can you not love me?
Here I am,
With my beautiful grain, soft as sable,
.....Your wonderful...kitchen table.

~ ~ ~ ~ ~

A message to myself

Don't analyse everything,
Take things as they are,
One at a time,
If they are not always as I wish,
Accept it gracefully.
Remember, Home is not work.
Listen to my heart,
It has never lied to me,
Keep at least one foot on the ground,
Everything will be fine,
.......Relax.....

In the realm of the unicorn

An Ageless....Mystical Island...
That Teems with fabled life...Floating in...
The Deepest Blue, ...In Intensity,
Surrounded by Thoughtfulness.....
...In Immensity,
An Ocean... Flowing with Kindness,
In...Mystery..... Timeless...
Rainbow'd Halo's,
Round Beautiful Pinprick'd Stars,..
...Being Tied together by Faeries,
Catching them when they Fall,
Flights of Resplendent Phoenix.
Magical Beings All.....
Constantly Reborn,
In a Maelstrom of Angel Dust, And Fireflies,
..All This Do I see...
...When I Look in Your Eyes.

~ ~ ~ ~ ~

So, you think you can read my mind!

You, thought yourself better, hah!

Now ....Over an hour has passed,

You'll not much longer last.

So, you think you can read my mind,

Oh......You're cool,

I'll give you that!

You're A cold, calculating, machine,

You think you can beat me,

That's where you're at!

Now that.... Didn't have me fooled,

At last..... overconfidence,

I'll take that!

You thought you had me then,

With that dispatched,

Though, the game is...My friend,

Just not where you think it's at.

GOTCHA!

Now That...Oh.... My hunger sate!

There's nothing you can do!

Your queen will now suffer the same cruel fate.....

....CHECKMATE...

~ ~ ~ ~ ~

Old nick's game

The devil stands at the table............

...Not just any heart, take this one.

I place the cup over it see.....Like so,

That's it,...

Now,.. watch carefully,... and,

Away we go.....

Round and round, this way and that,

Come play my friend,

Your sanity, I'll bend,

Wrong....

Hah Hah, It's not where you think it's at!

Play again?

Surely...Your spirit isn't broken yet!

Tut, Tut, don't call me names,

You need a good sense of humour,

If you're going to play with me,

At mind games.

~ ~ ~ ~ ~

Why?

OH, we talk, have known each other for years,
True, but, well, there's no "Personal" spark,
You're good looking, look after yourself,
You're smart.
So, how can it be?
You're sat there so close, with lovely smiles,
Yet, we're Worlds Apart!
And someone at distance,
Thousands of miles,
Never met, can be a good friend,
Kindred spirit, Dear heart.

~ ~ ~ ~ ~

A very special day

I see "Perfection",
Your hair, your eyes,
No deceit in disguise,
Even if nothing you say,
Your look, your smile,
Your beauty,
My spirit soars,
You really have made it for me,
A very special day.

~ ~ ~ ~ ~

What DO you want?

I'm Real, "Man", Not a token,
I'm a "What you see is what you get" type,
Of course I'll be open!
Yes, Transparent if you want too,
I'll make you safe!
Yeah, Yeah...Whatever you say,
Look,...
My job keeps the wolves away!
No..I've never on your business impinged!
Push me too hard though,
You might see me unhinged!
OK, I'll shut up, if you want me to.
I'll do whatever you want me to!
You want more?
C'MON, for Pete's sake,
I'm only a door!!!

~ ~ ~ ~ ~

About this poem:
Something we all take for granted, so for doors everywhere, ON behalf of the
rest of the human race....THANKYOU!! LOL xxx

It's my passion

There is so much negativity in the world
It's like,
A thick, cloying darkness, being unfurled.
Yet, In my world.... There is only light,
No trouble, No strife,
It can be difficult,
To make the unfeeling, understand,
Though sometimes, I have toiled hard,
Use mind and hand...I know where I'm at,
I feel I've never done a day's work in my life,
To create things, is my passion,
And will never, ever, stop doing that!

~ ~ ~ ~ ~

Stolen energy

A

red

drop

of my blood...

Your obsessive needy

behaviourism still dripping..

with my blood from your vampire

teeth always voraciously in lust for more

drenching yourself in the stolen energy you got

I feel my drained energy levels dropping to point zero

connecting to my power inside.......just until tomorrow

the vampire strikes again... ready to have his teeth

stuck once again into the flesh of my blood

when will you ever learn?...

Nothing is impossible

I know you're feeling a bit "Down",
Listen to me, don't frown,
You think it can't work,
It's all too far, too much,
Too precious,
Can't get near enough to touch,
Well, think on this for a while,
Believe in it, it'll make you smile,
If in your mind,
You live in the world of "Possible",
Nothing's Impossible, My friend,
So you will find.

Hand in hand

Always, you are on my mind,
Inside, you're clever, beautiful and kind,
You're absolutely gorgeous,
Modestly, you don't see.
I am over the moon,
To think, out of thousands,
You want me.
From Across the ocean,
Take my hand, Dear heart,
There's no distance between us now,
We're no longer apart,
And on life's wonderful journey, We'll set out
Happy together, forever, all throughout,
What an adventure we'll have,
All This I KNOW,
Without a shadow of a doubt !

In, or out

Once.....
When you were in, you were in,
When you were out, you were out,
So far away from it,
You couldn't hear it, truly, no doubt!
But now there's no excuse,
With mobile with you always,
It's in constant readiness for use!
Now,
You're always in,
Never out,
Unless later you want,
Some really serious,
Verbal abuse,
Oh…. Please don't shout!!

Poetry in motion

Poetry is Wonderful,
It's Therapeutic,
It's Mental, Psyche-illogical,
There's no short,
Nor long,
There's no right,
Nor wrong,
Pick up your pen, smile, have fun,
Or,
Write hurt,
Write love,
Be strong.

My dearest friend

I walked today, you were with me, I'm sure,
You're the Hawk hovering over Heather gorse,
You're the timeless waves, upon the shore,
Past and future, together, mixed must be,
To make "pure", present,
Transfixed on you and me.
Waves, wiping sand smooth,
Easing sombre mood.
Like giving a clean slate,
Encouraging us, new life writing to make.
Sometime in thought,
Spectre of past mistakes,
Of lessons learned, lessons taught!
With walk and think now done,
Past and future, tightly knit,
All Make our present,
To which I'll commit.
It's time my dearest friend, I'm ready now,
When you need me, I'll come.

~ ~ ~ ~ ~

The silly flea

Is it a twig?,
Is it a branch?,
I know! It's gotta be a tree,
It's so big an round,
I can run round it.....
....See?
Look it stretches alllll the way up,
All the way to...In-fin-ity,
An I know! It's not, just an enormous log,
"Oh, stop being a stupid flea,
Don't you know, can't you see?....
It's a hair of the DOG"!!!

Love over the air

When you're there, you're on.
When you're not, you're gone.
Simple as that!
Sharp as ball slapping bat.
First hot, then cold,
And up and down,
Not forgetting, the round and round.
We only use the written word,
later read it back,
feel embarrassed, absurd.
But, all that considered,
I still don't care,
I'm having a wonderful time,
With my interstate, transcontinental,
Thing over the air,
Cyber, love affair.

Tender moment

As you struggle, from one world to another,
All strength used,
One last, final push.
Pain, but, no abuse,
Left behind....
Blurred vision,
Future uncertain, to confront,
Held gently, then sleep,
Tenderness....
And Comfort, Find.

~ ~ ~ ~ ~

Dissolution

Disentangled entanglement of temporal spirituality,
Spreading, all part, yet apart,
Contracting spontaneity,
Life is,
That was, of no consequence,
Here time is void,
Meaningless.

~ ~ ~ ~ ~

The fool in the tarot deck

The Fool in the tarot deck-i wanna be....
with a bismuth yellow pony-tail blowing in the northern wind...
....flake white invisible faerie wings....
walking through pastures of viridian green,
take the quantum leap over the abyss!

Bare-feet under the African sky....
I still wanna play with my prussian blue painted words,
juggle them in the air of my astrological sign,
find a niche in the cresent moon...
and rest for awhile...

I still wanna watch the hippo's play in the zambezi for awhile...
paint under the arabian sun....on my way,
buy an umbrella for a wish for a day...
Roll with the woody hills in ixopo....

Cry at the ambassador tank....
Spraypaint and age the tuscan walls in fourways,
take the road less travelled by in Robert Frost's poem,
shed a tear or two...in the namib desert.

Cry at the burnt sienna sunset in the serengeti...
laugh at the baby elephants at kariba dam...
Encounter on my way... with the poor in zimbabwe...a day,
dress in a saffron robe in katmandu...

Walk the santiago de compostela....to find my soul,
paint the peak of uhuru on kilimandjaro in raw umber,
reach for the stars...
While hopping around on top of my painted world of art....

..In my bag over my free-spirited shoulder only....
a pencil...a brush.....
My winsor & newton cadmium yellow...
For in case my day turns blue.....
I CAN NEVER BE:
I can never be....
Your prefabricated mould....
Your pencil-sketched faerie chained to a cage....
Your sculpted Venus de Milo!

Your starry night van Gogh...
Your living expectation hung around my neck....
Your girl with the pearl earring in your Vermeer,
You abstract illusion....

my invisible painted faerie wings belongs to the wind...
No location...no space...no time....
Without my wings.
while alive...i would decay and die..!

The "Fool" 1

Embark on life's journey, unafraid,
You must believe, have utter faith.
All will be well,
This I know, for, I can tell, so solid,
On it, you can trade,
Don't worry, from all life's perils,
You will be safe.
With every experience, deep, essential,
Be, with knowledge gained, reverential,
Listen to the voluable,
For what may seem at first glance worthless,
Can be quite valuable.
Be a beginner, be the master,
Be the first, be the last,
From Alpha to Omega,
The equation of the Universe!
In final balance of opposites,
Be all twenty one parts of the Major Arcana.
Acomplishment, fulfilment, successful completion,
It's yours, if, with your heart you converse.
Be a free spirit, don't follow the herd,
Talk to your inner self,
You'll find all of this concurred,
Trust it, and, with lions heart,
Intuition and inner knowing,
You are one of a kind, a being apart.
Have undying belief that all will end,
Exactly as it should be,
Against this no-one can defend.
Face challenges, with energy, optimism and faith,
Start Upright,
Face new beginnings, not with haste,
You'll know all this true,
And to it relate!

The "Fool's" journey 2

My spirit wanders here, on my journey.
Free, unfettered, unbound,
By time, or distance,
Gifted, second sighted to infinity,
I hear only beautiful, heart sound.
Yet, my soul mate,
Spirit companion,
Still seeking, as yet, unfound.
There are, those that I have let come close,
Or, Near,
But, even as I hoped,
When, they saw the journey,
Recoiled, left me,
Because of fear.
But I will know you, when I find you,
You will know me,
You will take my hand,
Not look away,
Like me, unafraid, you will see,
And, together in spirit,
We will walk the land.

~ ~ ~ ~ ~

The tears of the "Fool" 3

My tears, Sometimes, Are for you,
Sometimes, They are for me,
Sometimes for joy, Happiness,
Sometimes, shared grief.
Never self pity.
My feelings for you,
Are, as in my belief,
Unshakeable, Untouchable, Yet felt,
Yes, even soft,
Rarely unsmooth, svelt,
I am, my spirit, with you,
Gliding peacefully, Watching over me,
Aloft.
For all colours Heard,
While, Seeing, All sound,
We two are seldom except, Momentarily,
When necessary,
Both feet, Earth Bound.
So that Order from Chaos,
Can be sifted, sorted,
New Wisdoms Found.
So on with my journey,
New places, New people,
In the hope, Perhaps,
Elusive thing, long sought after,
Will soon be found.
~ ~ ~ ~

About this poem:
The "fool" needs to be in communion with his spirit to find purpose, lead his life journey. though a journey that may seem to others at times to be chaotic, there is an order, xxx

A dream, (For "Peace")

In our World where,
More is less,
Less, can be more,
Up, is Rich,
Left is Poor,
Depending on your perspective,
Right is wrong,
From Your side of the fence,
From Your place in our human collective,
Where Might, IS right, we're stupid!
How, can Peace be Wrong?
As human race, winds itself up,
Til, almost snapping,
I hope, the brokers of peace will stop napping,
And, pray our spring is Strong!

~ ~ ~ ~ ~

The donger

It won't work without it,
Told ya, see!
Now I'm in a bind,
I've looked under the cushions,
I've looked behind.
When the big lottery comes on,
How will I know, if I have won the Wonga,
If I can't find, the damn TV donger?

~ ~ ~ ~ ~

Life in a goldfish bowl

In their own little world,

Round and round they go,

Sometimes so fast,

It makes the bowl vibrate, like man, really THROB

Why they do it, I really don't know.

Though...

One thing bout it I do,

The one in front is always ......

...Called...BOB.

~ ~ ~ ~ ~

Occam's razor

If something seems too complicated,

Cut it down,

Grind it Into small pieces,

Even desiccate it,

Sort it out,

Till all untangled, untwined,

Only then will you find,

Simplest answer is the truth,

It will tell you all,

That's Occam's Razor,

In principal.

~ ~ ~ ~ ~

I like you...

I like your life-is-a-celebration
I like your inspiration

I like your head-in-the-clouds-ideology
I like your philosophy

I like your nothing is impossible-theory
I like your story

I like your extra-ordinary-love-passion
I like your compassion

I like you...

~ ~ ~ ~ ~

The "Fool's" "Fool"

The wind whistles,
Dark befalls the land,
In my mind,
Sitting in front of a warm fire,
Holding your hand.
They say,
That if, you look into the embers,
You see only the past.
I look hard,
Take all that, mix it with present,
Now I can see, bright future at last.
Of a sudden,
I feel you near,
I see a hawk, hovering,
Soaring over heather gorse,
My friend!.... Most dear!
Never dear heart, will I, you fail,
Never your freedom can I curtail,
Vowed ,
Never to each other,
By mores of mortals, be bound,
I feel you take my hand,
To walk, in spirit, throughout all land,
You could have baulked,
Courage not found,
But, when you saw the journey,
You didn't look back,
You are unafraid!
Now is our time, my dearest friend,
Look at our path,
The future laid.

"Stormchild" (.......Supernature 1)

Seeming effortless,
As if with small intent,
First updraft caused,
Emptied lakes of content,
Concocted, boiling mist,
Of circled rainbows did consist.
Natural ingredients of no lack,
Huge anvil,
Whirling nimbus, dispersed cirrus,
All collected,
Coming storm, in eyes reflected,
Centers of obsidian black!
Together in friction,
Tossing fireballs, his predilection,
With mind focus,
Fork lightning crafted,
By high speed wind,
Boiled, cooled, wafted,
Stood 'stride mountain top,
Flying hair, arms raised,
Rain now streaming,
Gods of mayhem praised,
All calm commanded wild,
By supernature,
STORMCHILD!

~ ~ ~ ~ ~

Ocean and tea

I wanted to tell you, before you wake.....

...I dreamed a simple dream, of you and me,
Just sat on a beach somewhere, drinking tea,
Watching, Whales and dolphins,
In the ocean at play,
A dream is a dream, but then......
Who knows?......
...Someday.......

~ ~ ~ ~ ~

Not far......

You're far in miles,
Near in heart,
Close in mind,
In time, we're only an hour apart.
In my heart,
That's not far, it's near.
Only a short journey,
My friend, most dear!

~ ~ ~ ~ ~

Poetry, poetry

Ahhhhhh.

Poetry.....Poetry,

I don't know.....

It's like...

Do it yourself psychology.

Or..do I mean psychiatry?

It's good dredging mind for stuff,

But...

When it goes WRONG....

Oh....

Like self performed, full frontal lobotomy!

Then you think,

Enough is enough!

Oh......Just one more then,

I'll pick up my pen and write some STRONG stuff !

~ ~ ~ ~ ~

"H'Luanah" (.......Supernature 2)

Ocean laying calm,
Of windless balm,
Foaming, Gliding,
Skimming, Diving,
Speed in Concorde!
Gravity defying!
Forever flowing, Aura'd locks,
Shimmering.
Ghostly folded golden light,
Emotion, vigour, life,
Shining bright,
Changing hue,
Yet truly spoke,
Through eyes, deep of purest blue.
Like, acoustic, amplified,
Simplified, through depth,
Flick of tail,
Out of water leapt,
Beauty incarnate, in time, Pre-Dawn,
H'Luanah!
Not of mans story, through ages downlaid,
MERMAID!
Of Supernature borne

~ ~ ~ ~ ~

About this poem:
Second to stormchild, of the supernature trilogy

For Sabeel: painted friends filled with dreams

Little boy of four or five
with your happy face....
and a bowl with the
reflection of the moon.

I cant paint your picture..
Sabeel already did it on paper,
...instead
I can paint you a picture...

On canvas or paper,
of a mosaic of friends.
With the wisdom of sonofadam & spiritwalker,
in Renaissance Gold...

With the gentle softness of quietstorm,
In Rose...
With shhores enchanted spirit,
In Violet...

With poetengineers kindness,
In Naples Yellow...
With Andrew's humour,
In Bright Red...

and bentlee's integrity,
In Cremnitz White...
With trurorob's funny riddle,
In Carmine...

With yurima's compassion,
In Naples Yellow...
With walkerman's Grace,
In Copper...

With HotrodLarrys true heart,
In Yellow Ochre...
with stareintospace's bass clarinetist,
in Emerald...

With amahlala's magical bubbles,
in Cobalt Blue...
with pre_c48's footprints,
in Ultramarine...

with amanda09's brilliance in so. so! so?
in Pewter...
with nashnode's Violin Play,
in soft Charcoal Grey...

with Iiris's believe and beauty,
in Magenta...
with stressfree's Sail Today,
in Turquoise Light...

with boyshchrm6's mended heart,
in Terre Verte...
with anuna's sweetness,
in Lemon...

with passionatepoet's Nuptial Blessing,
In Indigo...
With moonlove's wish,
in Bronze...

so... you can remember all,
the friends
you made,
in the poet's corner....

And to remind you,
to follow that star...
And keep on,
Dreaming...

Look into your heart

Once you realise, it's a bit like....

Well.....

looking into your heart....

It's like...

Okay...

There are some that write,

There are those that don't,

Some think more, they don't hurt,

Some say more, they do hurt,

Some learn, and can,

others can't and won't.

~ ~ ~ ~ ~

A mistake

This language of ours is too clumsy,

So easy, a meaning or mistake to make,

Falsely seems, with eloquence adequate,

Dearest friends can great offence take,

With different minds,

Things can be lost in translation,

Made by accident, misunderstood,

With mistook intent,

True feelings by poet, really meant,

All for lack of information!

About this poem:

it can be so easy to say one thing, that by someone else is taken in a different way, both of course feeling in the right. All because this language although complicated, cannot always convey true thought.

we have all been there.....Andrew,......xxx

We laughed !

And, we laughed,
Not, in harsh joke,
But in gentle, pleasant comment.
Both easily amused,
Honesty, sincerely meant,
With no deliberate, contrived emotion used.
You listen, I talk,

In minds eye, a walk.

You talk, I listen,
Natural, of worries, no traces,
Our eyes, sparkle, glisten.
Big grins on faces,
Both, happy ourselves make.
Later, sitting together,
You sleeping, slight smile on your face,
I not moving, not wanting to make you wake,
Never wanting the evening to end,
You are always, and will forever be,
My very best friend.

~ ~ ~ ~ ~

You are a star !!

I
me
you..
they...
we are....
all the same..
each one of us unique
each one of us perfect in nature, of how-
-we should be...no mistakes...no imperfections...no flaws-
we are all part of the divine bigger picture-
serving each other.....
along the way
we are....
they...
you..
me
I

"Supernature" (.......Supernature 3)

With,
Past gentleness, for moment lost,
Speed of essence, at great energy cost,
Fury evolving, depths rising,
In proximity, no compromising,
Starting, a tower, of Enormity,
Of such conformity
So Miraculous,
Mermaid in circles,
Ever deeper!.....
Crafted water,
Life giving, Keeper,
So Mysterious,
Giant spout, she the Reaper
Now, at great speed!
Her at it's head maintained,
Lifted all from this world,
All it contained,
Aiming toward,
A greater need.!.......
....Whirling, Too
Ever increasing in speed,
Storm now ascendant,
Of his own volition,
Free will and need,
Taking all.
In ordered maelstrom.
In explosive emission

Transcendent,
Hot fission,
Comets, gather'd, sorted,
Atoms Smashed!
Chose for Excellence,
Moon tether'd, heavens moved, Gods exalted,
In violent benevolence,
All, with plasma, juggled ,mixed
Crushed together , then transfixed,
New world, where both will live,
Now created,
And did to H'Luanah give,
Wild now tamed,
World named,
Both elated!…..
….GAIA!
Now totally immersed,
With life, impregnated,
Sublime, Serene,
Full of energy, unabated,
Our Place,
Where SUPERNATURE, is supreme !

~ ~ ~ ~ ~

Rewind

STOP........
.....REWIND....ERASE...
All now DELETE.....
Face the future, teeth, grit,
Courage, Conviction,
FAST FORWARD.....Thinking,
New slate to be re-writ,
For New life to be COMPLETE!

~ ~ ~ ~ ~

The smile

In days of old,
When knights were bold,
And maids were free and willing,
One gave one, one,
Then the other, gave one, one,
Happy then, he gave her a shilling!

~ ~ ~ ~

Jamie Allen

18th-century darkhaired gypsylady….

cards spread out on a wooden table….

Dim light through 'e window pane:

"Jamie Allen, gypsy poet-piper…. young lad… playing ti the duke an' duchess an' earl….
wi the hangman an' the devil always on ya tail……. Jamie pack ya bags an' roam—

'fore ya become em prediction in em cards…….. em years of roguery 'ill catch up wi ya
'fore ya'd be chained ti ya lies …. Jamie pack ya bags an' roam-

serial army enlister an' deserter….. for Geordies shilling or two….
the devil an' the hangman on ya tail …. Jamie pack ya bags an' roam

where em rivers and fells set em stage for ya captures and escapes….
an' ya struggle ti survive along with em other lads….. Jamie pack ya bags an' roam-

stealing ya last Gatesheed steed… no jail can hold ya
…. ya'll end up in ya cell dying at seventy-five…. Jamie pack ya bags an' roam-

'fore em can sentence ya…. 'fore ya lamented cry be heard
through em lonely hawthorns wi 'em berries red an' thorns sharp…Jamie pack ya bags an' roam-

before ya become em prediction in em cards ….Jamie pack ya bags an' roam"

Into summer

Sun Shining......
Now fresh ....After rain,
Salt air, waves crashing,
Gulls calling, sand blowing,
Urge to travel,
Though, natural doubts,
I must first unravel.
Am I wishing? Only half knowing?
Hoping? Guessing?
Thoughts not properly flowing?
Like, after much joy,
Then missing it, then pain.
Almost panic,
I feel it growing, again!
Pictures in mind,
Sometimes, so far from reach,
All life lessons reviewed,
What to me, did they teach?
Don't let small problems, drag me down,
Live life with a smile,
It's easier than, with a frown,
And of the pain?
Take courage, take ticket,
For train boat or plane,
I've nothing to lose, and all to gain,
Forget how alone, I sometimes feel,
What used to make me cry,
I know me,
I know too, how with it, I must deal!

No more hesitation, just go!

Stop asking myself, will it work?

Because,

If I don't try! We will never know.

Now forgotten,

How in the past I've been burned,

Now for future, good thoughts,

I was lost for a moment,

But now,

My Happiness found..... Returned!

"Of you"

I was in winter,

It was bitter.

At the darkest hour, just before dawn.

Couldn't think, didn't know what to do,

When first I felt you in a gentle breeze,

Didn't know I was about to be re-born.

Saw honesty in words,

I found I could forget all pain,

Started to see beauty in simple things,

Felt as if life was a miracle, again,

All throughout my day.

I see you in the sunrise,

I see you in children, happily at play,

Before you, I was blind and couldn't see,

Even the deepest blue of the ocean,

The likeness of you,

Magnificence of mountains, or of tall, tall tree,

But, Now I do,

In all, of a beautiful pure, and the clearest simplicity

I like your way

I have to say,
I like your way,
It's goodness,
Itself, a gentleness,
Not harmful, pleasingly addictive,
Yet not presumptive, not predictive,
Nor of arrogance, or egotism, or unknowing,
With beauty of inner self, knowing.
It's clearly writ, in your manner,
How you wear it on your heart, like a banner,
Not liking shallowness, others imposing their will,
You know deep waters well, they're better and still,
Yet in prospect of hunt, always a thrill,
Love nature though, so never the kill,
Others think you have a complicated mind,
Seems to me, beautifully simple in kind,
Again to others, in person, always restless,
Often leaving situations, happily, with not more, but less,
It's what you do to live life at the crest,
You just know, simplest is best,
Keeping your own council, your privacy in accordance,
So publicly, in truth, you've no discordance,
Comfortable to be with, and, with what you are,
Truly humble, when people think you're a rising star,
Always striving for that just out of reach shelf,
Looking for knowledge, knowing the truth, not kidding yourself,
It all rings through, clear as a bell,
For those that know, and can tell,
And, in your own way, like me,
In the view of most others, a complete anomaly!

In confusion

WOT……..With,

Looking before……..regrets after….

…..In time….

Wouldn't touch it with yours….

Let alone mine…..

Washing your hands…..Under ladders…..

walking the line…..

In tatters...

...before leaping……opening doors….

Isn't it confusing….

…..life….

When you're mixing Metaphors!

~ ~ ~ ~ ~

Tough love, no nonsense !

Want to survive?

Which then?

Dead or alive?

Life is for living,

Giving up, is slow dying,

Optimism and hope,

That's got to be your "Dope",

See for yourself, I'm not lying!

~ ~ ~ ~ ~

About this poem:

forwards is a good direction to go, I think!……andrew….xxx

Spooky but groovy

We were part of a star once,
And then once again,
Particles sharing everything,
We both resonate to sing,
Of Love, joy and pain,
Spooky but groovy, because one day,
We will be again.

~ ~ ~ ~ ~

We,....... the Ark

We.......The Ark,

Plummeting through the dark,

At an appalling pace,

Passing stars, no name nor place,

Multi faceted jewels hanging in space,

Though once behind us, there is no trace,

This, is our time in hyper drive,

Hum of just engines and dampers, keeping us alive,

Rings of Saturn, now three months past,

On a journey that ten years will last,

Colours haloing ship, put northern lights to shame,

Folding time and space, engineers claim,

Said goodbye to our home,

All friends and relatives we had known,

They've all been dead now for years,

Before we left, we shed our tears,

We have to think like that, we're not out of line,

It's all to do with theory of light speed and time,

Seems like an everlasting journey into night,

Hope our new home will sustain us, scientists say it might,

And when we arrive as pioneers,

For different reasons, we will once again shed tears,

For our sun is dying, turning in colour from yellow to tope,

So we thousand few, really are mankind's last hope!

Playing the game

At school………
I, was the scourge of the lower fourth,
Even, turned round the weather vane on the roof once.
So south pointed north.
I really was a healthy, young mischievous pup,
I loved chemistry,
Always looking for new ways to blow things up.
I'd sneak up behind girls,
While they were talking at play,
"Twanging", or undoing bra straps, one handed,
While pretending to look the other way.
Then....To be a real pain,
Stealthily, pulling down one of their socks,
So they'd have to bend over, to pull it up again.
Loved swimming for our team at fast pace,
And cross country running too,
Slower, but a much longer race.
And when came my very last day,
Purloined head masters gown up the flagpole,
When I left was he sorry?
I Didn't stick around long enough to hear him say!
Now, all grown up, still doing the same,
Though now, more metaphorically,
With the cards I've been given, still playing the game!

Well I never

In a short time we've come so far,
From bicycle, to atom bomb to motor car,
Global warming, crops failing,
Millions starving, cos, it's stopped raining,
Well I never,......
.....Arn't we marvelous and,
So very, very, clever!

~ ~ ~ ~ ~

Memory from my schooldays
Author: Anonymous

There was a young man from dill,
Who swallowed an atomic pill,
His bellybutton corroded,
His Arsehole exploded,
And they found his balls in Brazil!

~ ~ ~ ~ ~

About this poem:
Strange, some things one remembers.......lol....andrew...xxx

The space between.......

Here, it's dark,

Here, even the sun fails to rise,

Not even the lark.

Winter seems but a step away,

Having tasted ,

Savoured,

Cherished, ...

Nothing wasted.

Devine, peacefulness,

Bitter peel, inner sweetness,

Be still, my brother,

It's just the nothing space,

Between closing one door,

Then, opening another.

~ ~ ~ ~ ~

We,....... the Ark 2

Some ten years now have passed,
We're in orbit round our new home at last,
Not like what we left behind,
Half dessert, half snow, to make you blind,
No......This is of a different hue,
Shades of green, but mostly blue,
We look in wonder at what we see,
Oceans and clear, blue, blue sea,
And, clean air to breath,
Atmosphere, doesn't with hot volcanic ash seethe,
Strange plants and trees, with beautiful fruit,
Peaceful people like us, this place will suit,
But, what do we call it, what's in a name?
We can't call it after home, it's not the same,
As we move to the world, our ship in orbit will stay,
Though not for much longer, it's metal is full of decay,
With naming, much argument, and did it compound,
Til a child thought of an old word.........Earth.....
Meaning, ground!

~ ~ ~ ~ ~

Ever constant

It felt like winter in my soul,
A kind of twilight, had taken hold.
An all pervading greyness,
No warmth, unnatural, paralysing cold,
Bleak as bleak, misery untold.
For many a day, week,
Month, year.
Something, then felt, rather than seen,
That, you were near.
An inner glowing,
Somehow, a knowing,
All would be well,
I could just tell, and ever growing.
Soul re-building, making,
Toward my awakening,
And ever since, with my soul conversant,
Indeed, you really are, my Friend most Dear,
And, In my mind, Ever Constant.

~ ~ ~ ~ ~

You took the moon

I offered you a sip of life's nectar,
You drank greedily,
You laughed,
I became your provider, your protector.
I gave you the wind,
You wanted more, You took the rain,
Laughed, then left me,
I gave you the moon,
You promised me love again,
You laughed again, I couldn't see,
Didn't want to know you'd cause more pain,
Lies and the truth bend,
No pretence, no more pretend,
Now You've untied that sacred knot,
I must be strong, This must be the end.

~ ~ ~ ~ ~

A time to let go...

I found the little fragments...
Of your innocent soul laying compliant inside the silence of the moments....
...Inside the rifled cardboard box of our existence together - unpacked today...
Drizzling as the soft rain outside my window – my melancholic inner mood on
display.

I prayed for an angel on my path....
"My angel sent" - you manifested in the form of my child - a heavenly sworn
oath,
an aura of quietness and unconditional serenity...born with Buddha-nature,
acoustics to my empty void -you became part of my reason for tomorrow's
signature.

Simple decorative naive words from a little 9-year old daydreamer with a red
heart at play,
your dedication when your dad's soul left, dancing all over the love letters on
mothers-day...
Your designs in brilliance... predicaments of what was to become written in
stone,
experiments of the chemistry of life written and jotted down... alone.

Molecules, carbohydrates, lipids and nucleic acids, on folded paper...
The remains of our cardboard-existence together, becomes the H_2O from my
eyes later.
The branched river of tears found its way onto the round-bottom flask and
broken glass,
the old physics handbook and photos with yellow corners now a time....pass!

The run-out sanded hourglass of adolescence suggest the time to let you go -
on your way to independence and adulthood....you go.
Fly free my angel - the empty-nest syndrome arrives at my door,
I will love you forever – my days without you...leaving me poor...

Finding my reflection

Detached, submerged, twirling,

Round and round, sideways swirling,

Seeking my reflection,

Since my souls affection,

Chance meeting,

Too quickly gone, memory fleeting,

Easing, aching, wanting free,

You alone have the key,

Be I awake or asleep,

The secret way you keep,

So in spirit my hand you'll take,

Holding, guiding pencil, drawing make,

Fine lines together, in thought, weaving,

For any that would harm us, so deceiving,

Fiction and reality,

Future in history,

Self conscious in mind,

Present through absence, of a kind,

Through relevance of purpose,

Possibility raised in subconscious,

Falling slowly over distance,

Unsure at times, of my own existence,

Through destiny, tumbling,

Lost thought of self, how humbling,

Like of water, though not wet,

Of unfathomable depth,

Not fighting,

Currents pulling,

From far distance something shining, refracting

Recognising, pure light, You, attracting,

Illuminating the way, safely forward,

Round seeming rocks and spikes toward,,

Soft heaven, then ascension ,

Melding, blending, until,

You and I are We, and, of our own dimension.

We,....... the Ark 3

Some years have now passed,

I'm old now, time for me to rest at last,

On our voyage through time, on eternities ledge we perched,

Finely balanced, looking over the precipice, fearing a fall if we lurched,

And, on our return, for traces of our old civilization, we searched,

Found nothing, time it seems had us erased,

In a way, it made it easier, for the future we faced,

And, in the future, it will seem as though,

Man just appeared, for the truth they won't know,

One once proud continent is now five,

The diaspora has begun, now we know we will survive,

I write here from Africa, as we have named this place,

Now, our children travel, to find on this earth, their own special place,

In a small canister from the ship, I now bury this deep in the sand,

Hoping the elements, to it will be kind, and,

For it to be found,

For the truth to be known about our Earth.....

Why we called it ......Ground !

Plastic surgery....

So, you want plastic surgery?
Not happy with your face?....Hmmmm lets look,
Well, I can tell you, there's no need, believe me,
For that few grand , bank withdrawal you took,
Just use this muscle and this, that's it, copy me,
This is what's called a smile,
It can transform you, do you see,
Take it away, Try it....It's free...

~ ~ ~ ~ ~

A little magic

AAAALLLLLAA.....kaZZZZam......."Pooof"!,

Well, there you go Princess,
One ugly frog, now Princely man,
Just hope with this transmogrification,
Comes, much wanted love action,
And, That on your wedding night,
All his bits work, to your satisfaction........

~ ~ ~ ~ ~

My first real car

My dad said it was a wreck, a jalopy,
Don't know, but it took all my pocket money,
It was a Ford something or other,
Opened drivers door, pulling one thing, pushing another,
At each corner, a flat tyre,
Each one bald and sprouting wire,
Radiator leaked like a font,
What more could any boy want?
The bucket seats were a dream,
Velour, I think once coloured cream,
The clocks went backwards,
When it went forwards,
Engine missed when it run,
But, taking it apart was so much fun,
And putting together, again and again,
Never ran again,
Only paid twenty for it,
What a bargain….
Only Cost thirty to scrap it!

~ ~ ~ ~ ~

Ithaca

Author: Constantine Cavafy (1863-1933)

When you set out on your journey to Itacha,
pray that the road is long,
full of adventure, full of knowledge.
The Lestrygonians and the Cyclops,
the angry Poseidon-do not fear them;
You will never find such as these on your path
if your thoughts remain lofty, if a fine
emotions touches your spirit and your body.
The Lestrygonians and the Cyclops,
the fierce Poseidon you will never encounter
if you do not carry them within your soul,
if your heart does not set them up before you.

Pray that the road is long.
That the summer mornings are many, when,
with such pleasure, with such joy
you will enter ports seen for the first time;
stop at Phoenician markets,
and purchase fine merchandise,
mother-of-pearl and coral, amber and ebony,
and sensual perfumes of all kinds,
as many sensual perfumes as you can;
visit many Egyptian cities,
to learn and learn from scholars.

Always keep Ithaca in your mind.
To arrive there is your ultimate goal.
But do not hurry the voyage at all.
It is better to let it last for many years;
and to anchor at the island when you are old,
rich with all you have gained on the way;
not expecting that Ithaca will offer you riches.
Ithaca has given you the beautiful voyage.
Without her you would never have set out on the road.
She has nothing more to give you.

And if you find her poor, Ithaca has not deceived you.
Wise as you have become, with so much experience,
you must already have understood what Ithaca means.

Seek and you shall find

You've searched the world,
But, you're still not found,
With your head above the clouds,
Both feet, firmly to ground.
Hear all the lofty talk,
But, learn nothing new,
Taking care where you walk,
Now getting older,
Still looking for you!
Stop for a minute, think,
From font of inner self,
Take a long cool drink,
Look inside your mind,
You've really been "There", all the time,
So, seek less, you might then,
"You", find!

~ ~ ~ ~ ~

About a poet

To others, we are complicated people,
To us, we are simple people,
But something we don't understand,
What is it about us, others can't understand?

~ ~ ~ ~ ~

The very best.....

The Sun shines for us, wherever we are,
Through beautiful minds poetry, near and far,
Like two children, in a field at play,
Making daisy chains, jumping in the hay,
We have rainbows for skipping ropes,
Both our hearts, soaring with hopes,
The silver raindrops, upon which we dance,
Make us dare to take our life's chance,
Tonight, we'll swing from the stars and the moon,
Making as we go, such a happy tune,
And when our play is done,
After having so much fun,
In each others arms, we'll contentedly rest,
Dreaming of tomorrow, of all good things, the very best.

~ ~ ~ ~ ~

Of nature

You, are of the sun when rising,
Life giving, always compromising,
And, of the clouds and rain,
Nourishment, joy, sometimes pain,
When pushed too far, disaster too,
Yet repair yourself of mans deeds, you do,
And, though we have tried since we came,
The wise of us know, you will never be tame!

~ ~ ~ ~ ~

Of life.......

With chest round the ankles,
Interfering with bangles,
With short shorts,
Ignoring others' retorts,
To emoticons addicted,
What's saying next is not predicted,
With verses shallow,
Like chocolate coated marshmallow,
Am I being fair? Or is there,
Really nothing between the ears, but air!

~ ~ ~ ~ ~

Mirror mirror on the wall...

Miror mirror on the wall...
who's the prettiest maiden in town????
Oh please pleeeeeeeze tell me its me...
i need your assurance twenty four-seven...
What about my eenie -teeie-weenie
Yellow polka dot bikini.....???
it fitted once- upon- a -time...
My worlds falling apart since
my lover no 61 left....
I know I was Cinderella once upon
a time....but pleeezeeeeeee
Whisper a lie to me... in my ear
That i'm still the prettiest maiden in
town....

Maybe gravity took its toll
after the last baby was born...???
but i still need to hear you lying
to hear for ever.....
That i'm the prettiest maiden
in town....
pleeeeeeeeze erase
the wrinkles around my face
and the bags under my eyes
with your magic wand.....or
use photoshop...if you wish
anything now, will do....
Pleeeeeeze let me drown inside
my pool of narcism
because i need lover no 62 to
help pay the bills at
the end of the month...
and to forget that i'm 45....

~ ~ ~ ~ ~

Love life......

The sun is rising.
Mist form'd, now dissolving,
Yesterdays sins absolving,
Plan for today, now forming,
Compromising,
Hope, comprising,
Love of life, complete,...Advising!

~ ~ ~ ~ ~

Of love.......

Why do you ask, what does it mean to be in love?
When asked, some mutter, something about hand and glove,
Like they're almost ashamed to admit,
That people might think them some kind of "Twit",
But different as a bird walking, to flying on the wing,
Love, they say, changes everything,
So for what it is, let it be named,
Take it for what it is, don't be ashamed,
Itself, it keeps changing, from one minute to next,
No hard and fast rules, no following text,
What's right today, can be wrong tomorrow,
Happiness can turn to sorrow,
Then Sure as a rainbow, following rain,
Change back again,
Fear not, it's not an illness, just a hormonal thing,
Both learn to compromise, and in unison, you'll sing,
So then, you don't want a cure for this infection, of affection?
Well then, don't be silly,
Just accept things as they are, and don't ask the question!

Of distance........

Why worry about distance,
It is finite,
When you can be there in your mind,
The power of which,
Is infinite!

~ ~ ~ ~ ~

Voyagers

By night, steering by star,
Keeping going, travelling near and far,
Wandering all the sea,
By day, following the sun, that's me,
Disasters have me befell,
The stories, my friend, like you I could tell,
Hoping for a fair wind behind,
Calm waters, elements kind,
I sailed on, hoping, you I would find,
Following a course, long set in my mind,
Then, one stormy night,
The wind, whipping up waves, with might,
I saw you, struggling like me,
Against a cruel, cruel sea,
Both being pitched and tossed,
We were nearly lost,
I fought til I came along side,
What I saw, made me know with you I'd abide,
Forever, together, sailing side by side
Upon life's sea,
For, Voyagers are we!

Love's sweet embrace......

So many years had I wandered lost,
Until at last, pre-ordained, our paths crossed,
Then like magic, you were in my life,
Soon banished was all trouble and strife,
With gentle mind.
Your sense of humour like mine,
We talk and talk,
In our minds, we walk,
Hand in hand,
Upon the sand,
Both minds in tune,
As nature intended, under the stars and moon,
Forgetting forever, time and place,
Spending our time in love's sweet embrace.
~ ~ ~ ~ ~

"Home"

Forever, in it's place,
Revolving in space,
Not too near to the sun, not too far,
Looking blue and peaceful from afar,
A beautiful jewel so rare, no other can compare,
Against black backdrop, hanging there,
On her journey, though not alone,
For us mere humans, our wonderful home!
~ ~ ~ ~ ~

Dreadlocks Rod and happiness

I remember him sitting next to me...
Resting for a while...
in the shade,
far away from home,
asking for a drag of my cigarette...
My self-acclaimed son...
"Ma, i hate this place-it sucks,
being so far from home..."
"I'm telling you-can't take it
no more.....
"Rod, have you been happy...
When you were back home?"
"Oh no!-the ol' man gave me hell-
even worse than this-telling ya"...
"Had to run away few times..."
..."You see rod, if you're not content
with who you are,
you'll never be content,
where you are."
He looked at me,
put the cigarette butt out,
in the sand,
with his safety boot...
Placed a kiss
on my cheek,
and with
a "Thanks ma,"
stood up,
and walked
away...
I kept on wondering....
if Rod will find
his happiness?

From the crucible

Who was this mere mortal?
Poet daring to open the portal,
Who had by ancient text learned,
And, in sacred crucible, precious elements burned,
When mixed,
Then with rare metals, transfixed,
Now a circular vortex forming,
Plasma, flame transforming,
Motes like fireflies arose,
Apparition like, hair, face, eyes and nose,
As poet looked on, on bended knee,
Beautiful body appeared, as he could see,
Aura of colours all around,
Lending way to hypnotic sound,

Swirling smoke, heat and flame,
More substance did she gain,
To be poets fiery arrow,
To fly straight and true over minds that are shallow,
Lighting all dark in her wake,
Poetry, through eloquence and fire to make,
Reborn of flame,
All true poets, know her name!

About this poem:
Brigid.....goddess of fire, war and poetry.....worshipped by poets long ago.........

The poet and Arawn

While in heaven, bored gods threw a dice,
To decide the fate of man and mice,
Poet had a story to tell,
Though with it went, if told, an eternity in hell,
So Goddess of poets, fire and war, did he summon, truth to tell,
To ring it out loud, clear as a bell,
For he with Arawn, King of Otherworld,
Struck a bargain, so the story unfurled,
Poet, had accidentally killed Lord of Death's hound,
Now, said king wanted poets flesh, though more than a pound,
So, to save his life,
And plenty of strife,
He, and he were to change places,
And have different faces,
For the Lord needed poet's body in war to fight,
No use poor poet, being contrite,
For as sure as Arawn's hounds ran through the autumn sky,
If he didn't agree, he would surely die.

~ ~ ~ ~ ~

Ethelgorn and Cromm

Ethelgorn stood on a golden beach of sand,
Looking out to sea from land,
Leaning on sword,
Far horizon, looking toward,
Then wearily, on hillock sat, sighed, rested,
Watching restless waves, windblown, crested,
All observed by God's, reflected in black of ravens eye,
Mans fate to come, time soon nigh,
He, thinking of tomorrow,
Of Gods power that he must borrow,
Thinking of magick of ancient tongue,
Meant only for Kings, not commoners or those among,
Zend once from Sanskrit,
Later which on stone, will once more be writ,
Too long past, in mists of time to trace,
Cromm, bower of the mound, God fallen from grace,
Him, will he call forward to fight,
So to make wrongs done, turn to right,
Fighting planned on foot, all hand to hand,
To see who will rule this fair land,
Ten thousand men, on Olde Englands side,
Against him ten thousand or more, over mountain did hide,
If he wins, true King will he be appointed,
Battle first though, before he's anointed,....
....So, the Gods game pieces on a board are now set out,
Who will win? Victory claim and freedom shout?
To the Gods in boredom, only a game to play,
To man below, skin and blood soon to pay.

~ ~ ~ ~ ~

Battle's eve

The sky turned to dark from pale,
Freezing rain and ice like rocks began to hail,
Hammer against anvil of cloud,
Caused thunder frighteningly loud,
Startled animals, sheep and cattle,
That night, even the bravest heart did rattle,
While in one camp, slave for sacrifice was coldly stoned,
In the other, metal pointed ends to poles lashed, axes honed!
The Gods make self amusement of a kind,
Not easily understood by human mind,
They are simple, not complicated,
Though lack of feeling, should never be underestimated,
While dead slave at foot of mountain is lain,
Gods are playing each other, advantage to gain,
And even Cromm, Arawn and Brigid, though Gods by name,
Will be found to be mere pawns in this higher game!
Now, the Gods are almost ready to play,
While twenty thousand men, asleep in battledress lay,
Some will march over mountain in clothes sodden,
While for others down below, stinking bogs will have to be trodden,
All the time, Arawns hounds on leashes strained,
Smelling death to come, still to hells gate chained.

~ ~ ~ ~ ~

Battle of Arawn and Cromm

It was just after first light,
Two armies facing each other, time to fight,
Crowd in heaven now gathered round,
Excitement, wine and mirth and musical sound,
Eagerly watching game board,
For battle, coming of time toward,
We watch with them, the story unfold,
For in the future, a fable to be told,
All captured by raven, from it's eye.
Under leaden sky,
Two armies facing each other, standing by,
Each, swords and pikes on shields rattled,
Each man free born, hardened, battled,
At the head, standing in front of each,
Arawn and Cromm, wanting the other a lesson to teach,
Disguised as men,
But each as big as ten,
So, lord of death itself, life to confound,
Against Cromm, previously fallen, bower of the mound,
Then of a sudden, in Heaven and Earth a mighty roar,
As signal is given to start the war,
On message from Arawn,
Poet did unleash hounds this very dawn,
To run amuck, round up the souls of both living and dying,
Gods in heaven, laughing with delight, now almost crying,
Pieces on the board falling,
On earth, men wounded, dying, crawling,
Cromm spun up a mighty whirlwind, picked up all weapons that fell,
Hurled them with all might at Arawn, god of hell,
Hounds, in the blink of an eye, coming to his relief,
At defiant speed, catching all from whirlwind, in hells teeth,

Collateral fallout was so quick, so much,
Took time for Lord of Death, all souls to touch,
While on earth men died, souls pained,
Gods laughed and drank at each advantage gained,
Then when battle reached critical tempo,
Of a sudden it happened, not even gods how, did know,
Appeared in middle of whirling wind,
Brigid, who did all harm recind,
And with the mighty strength of a Gods arm,
Commanded an almighty calm!……
Now though a God can change place with man,
There is only one that with a God can,
And that is dreamweaver, as you know,
For he shall never of himself show,
Now, with ire he gathered all unearthly matter,
Did Gods and game board angrily scatter,
Because he had seen previously all that was meant,
Brigid, not as thought by Poet summoned, but by dreamweaver sent,
Banished forever Arawn to hell, no more earthly souls to confound,
Promoting Cromm now to master of the mound,
Then with a touch so gentle, Brigids soul did he hold,
Made her mortal, with eyes blue and hair of gold,
Made space fabric bend, borrowed time,
Gave to prince and princess, in another existence line,
Brought them here to yesterday,
Giving them a chance to make their own way,
And all from beginning to end,
Ethelgorn, a Knight will he make him, for her honour to defend,
Somewhere between past, present and future, inextricably linked,
All borne in mind by dreamweaver's subtle instinct.

~ ~ ~ ~ ~

"Hawk", a poet's interlude....

The waves are crashing,
Battering old pier, still standing,
Gulls crying,
Fishers wading,
The wind, almost a gale,
The sky dark, in patches, light blue, in contrast, pale,
On the slope, riding the up draught,
I saw, then laughed,
My hawk had returned,
Not been seen since the heather gorse had been burned,
High headwind, she hung in the air,
All I can do is stop and stare,
For minutes, just seeming motionless, like on sky painted,
Then, of a sudden, to the left she fainted,
Slight twitch of tail, and up,.... She's soaring
No-one could say watching this, is boring,
Now, at really high speed,
Diving vertically, as of need,
Making her kill, then still,
In fluid flight, climbing away, back up the hill,
And once again, out of sight........
Only now, do I think and stop,
I have my camera with me......I just forgot!.......

~ ~ ~ ~ ~

Knight of hope....

Eyes of deepest blue, flowing blonde hair, tied neatly,
Took her place next to father, king, smiling sweetly,
Sat on podium seeming composed, relaxing,
Seeming nothing on her mind too taxing,
Breasts heaving gently, beneath white silken dress,
Knowing the knight was there, her to impress.
She hadn't seen his face yet, as is customary, a must,
But knowing by his manner, in him she can trust,
Tying her cloth heart to his sleeve as he asked,
She his mission told to him, tasked,
Then she with dared hope of winning,
Feeling true love will emerge, no longer thought of sinning,
He, pledged allegiance, knelt to pray,
Quietly, that, her love for him be won this day,
She, now in excitement, barely contained,
As attempts at being royal princess, seemingly maintained,
Yet with eyes afire ,expression flushing,
Heart beating wildly, breath in short bursts gushing,
He, now rising, left hand, sword hilt clasping,
Right fist clenched, touching heart and chest, in saluting,
Then, turning smartly, steps to horse counting,
Engaged help of page friend, his white charger mounting,
As She watched him, to the end of the field he trotted,
She had to herself admit, her heart was taken,......
She was indeed besotted...

~ ~ ~ ~ ~

The darkest of knights.....

Queen of all that's black over fair,
Queen they say, of all darkness and air,
With long red hair, in tresses hung
Most wicked witch, since time begun,
Had seen knight of hope and princess dear,
Before it happened, in enchanted mirror, she kept near.
There and then formulating her evil, cunning plan,
To end their destiny, even before it began,
Decided she would battle princess's good knight,
To the death, though not in fair or good fight,
A magick suit of armour and sword, that's what she needed,
Wove spells of immediacy and to Gods of Dark pleaded.
Upon happening, most evil spell, opened the Portal,
It had never been done before, by mere witch, half mortal,
Reached through to find Lord of Underworld's spore,
Pluto, who of all things dark, commanded the law,
And whereupon he sat on Obsidian throne,
Guarded by Gorgon of same, that turned Atlas to stone,
And thereupon avoiding it's gaze,
Agreed bargain with Dark God through magick haze.
And after signing away her soul, agreeing to pay the price,
Closed Portal, and, was back to Earth in less than a thrice,
Thus first, with Cloak of Invisibility worn,
Did herself with magick armour and sword adorn,
Then to Tournament did go, with confidence made,
That she had dug Good Knight's grave with magick spade.
But, what she didn't know and couldn't tell,
When she the Portal made, with wicked spell,
The very smallest of ripples in space did it make,
And, to dreamweavers keen senses it loudly spake!

~ ~ ~ ~ ~

Battle for destiny

The dream weaver watched, unseen,
With critical eye, all observing, keen,
As princess sat, bosom heaving,
Good Knight for far end of the field was leaving,
Stood off, to one side, on hillock, grassed,
Dark witch lurked, Evil incarnate, unsurpassed,
Gloating in mind, that good Knight, will soon breath his last,
While adjusting sword, enjoying thought of coming task,
Deepest black ravens, circled overhead,
Chilling minder of things to come, and the dead,
Weaver, mind made up, Princess and good Knight, to defend,
Time and distance, did HE now bend,
Summon'd two Gods, for ALL are his subjects too,
Venus and God of War, to help good Knight his battle to do,
Goddess of love then cast a spell,
All around princess, so all would remain calm and well,
Mars, good Knights armour and sword did touch,
Gave it magic properties, equal to dark Knight's, as much,
On horses now then at opposites, end to end,
Good Knight, eager to win and to princess his love intend,
Dark Knight waiting for trumpets to sound,
So she their destinies could confound,
Then from silence, first trumpet did sound,
Huge roar from crowd erupted from all around,
Then all trumpets blared,
Promising, glory to the victor, because they had dared,
On this signal for tournament to begin,
Lances at the ready, spurs dig in,
Both horses, now knowing, it had begun,
Steeled themselves, then toward each other at full pelt run,
First contact, simultaneous, as lances struck,
Both splintering hugely, forcing both Knights, at full gallop to duck,
Then galloping on to opposite end,
Each, now swinging swords, for near future to kill and defend,
Then tight at fields end, did horses turn,

Pulled up sharp, while each rider weighed up return,
Then, good Knight let out battle cry,
At the same time, Wicked Witch, spied two Gods with her magic eye,
Knew instantly with regret, good Knight would not today die,
And, that her own hour was almost nigh,
Now, together again, joined in battle, tempo faster paced,
Each Knight knowing destiny was now being faced,
Now, good Knights armour and sword from Mars on loan,
Seemed to take on a life all of it's own,
Saw a weakness, witches eye slit in armour, though by magic defended,
Not strong enough, so, this is how her existence shall be ended,
Sharp sword then, like lightning struck,
Whole body heaved then did buck,
And as she fell from her horse to ground,
Disgusted onlookers to their horror found,
Green mess oozing from armour throughout,
And acrid smoke curling from helmet, of evil origin, no doubt,
......Then soon after, throughout the land,
Proclaimed Royal marriage, of promised princess's hand,
And many happy years will they live,
As they honour each other, and themselves to each other give,
Both hearts rejoicing out loud,.......
.......Then Returning.......
Sky.....
Of dawn grey cloud, Suddenly echoes round mountains so loud,
Appeared...Circled hole in space fabric,
Coloured, etched, by blue green electric,
Out worldly in content,
Two crystals seen first, for dream world meant,
Then, snout aflame, eyes red embered,
Unearthly Scream of air being rendered,
And look, riding on back by giant wing,
Seeming of man, riding...coaxing,
As if in exultation,....wand, upward holding,
Commanding timespace, behind now, collapsing, folding,
While round crystal orbs playing,
Lightning rings, crackling, cooling,

Wing beat slowing, now gliding,
Emerged near to eyrie, on thermal rising,
Dragon exhausted, at end of flight,
To rest, to ready, again for tonight!

The Devil and me...

"No external condition can ever be stronger than my internal state of mind"
and then just,...just when I'm dancing on safe ground territory...of a kind...

the devil knock's on my door....
tap-dancing on my floor..........
"Defeat me if you can" : says he,
"I have my perfect – strategy....,"
"I'll have you cry for an elegy...."
your weakness is mine.... at last
"I'll let you re-live the past........"
"I'll take you back to the cardboard-boxes stored in your cob-web subconscious
mind"
"I'll take away your freedom of choice and.... let you become forever enslaved to
mine"
"I'll rob you of your future experiences and leave you in the pathetic corner to
bind..."
"I'll have you to dwell in my harms"
"I'll let you shiver in my arms"......
"I'll have you chained to me".........
"I'll.... keep you imprisoned in me"
"I'll whirl you inside my vortex"...
"I'll cover your soul with darkness"
"I'll send my ghost as your wife"..
"I'll own your soul for.......... life"
"I'll be your creation....... as long"
.... as you want me to be"
Snarl the devil with the name:
..................-FEAR-...................
No glory.......................no fame
My own self- limitation............
My own self-creation..............

The Genie in the lamp

you look into the lamp,at the flame
see something in there, in life's game
you've seen it before, but you just can't place
wistfulness, now written all over your face
when someone thinks you settled
has you on a chain, heavily metalled
doesn't matter how long the length
it's like a millstone sapping strength
genie does then your mind invade
undoes all plans, others in your name have made
as you pack your bags in sorrow
thinking of their pain tomorrow
thanking god for the voice
now giving you a choice
and after you've gone, how they'll rage
but you can never be held in a cage
of you, they were too demanding
no matter how you explained,
they remained not understanding
so look into the lamp
mental chains, yourself unclamp
ask your wish, with happy heart, motives pure
the genie will grant it one day...that's for sure!

A new chapter

We've had many a storied leaning,

Of people or mystical being,

A dragon that flies,

Beautiful faerie, with deepest blue eyes,

Even, a kind and gentle unicorn,

New poems, lovingly delivered, healthily born,

But now real life, with all interlaced,

Past, present and future, have all been faced,

Journey of fool, with poetry as his tool,

Found and woo'd his own sweet fool,

With, hand, reaching hand,

Cross oceans, land to land,

Much mirth, joy and tears,

Banishment of oldest fears,

All with love, polished and linished,

This small life chapter is almost finished,

But don't worry, We're not thinking of leaving,

We've so much to do, lots more dream weaving,

So to hell with the devil,

We're going to take it to the next level,

With, new stories to be told,

Maybe with princess's and knights of old,

And as we may need to earn a shilling,

Maybe too, of maids young, free and willing,

And thinking anew, another look,

I sense, in the air, a lovely book,,

So, like with cricket, a second inning,

A new chapter is just beginning

We'll have so much to say, have loads of fun,

It's already, while you sleep, been begun,

Ideas like pheasants, HAH!

We're gonna shoot 'em, hang 'em and bag 'em,

Just you watch, while we make, The Impossible happen !

Elidor

On leaving,
It's deceiving
Looks like a plain brick wall,
Yet in this reality, not like at all,
For if you stand here at a certain time of day,
When the sun's about half way up, though it's hard to say,
Then, the old gypsies violin,
Grasp firmly by neck, put body under chin,
Draw firmly, but smoothly, over strings with bow,
Then a single note will play and seem as though,
It could turn a rainbow to sound,
Your heart will start to pound,
A strange vibration will everything, overtake,
Causing the very ground to move and shake,
The wall will begin to fade,
As if of fresh air made,
Then with the start of a shimmer,
You'll catch a glimmer,
Of the secret way, the very door,
To the realm of the Unicorn,
Fabled land of ELIDOR

CONTENTS

Life's greatest gift
In the beginning
dreamweaver
Dragon
While there is hope there is everything
A place called home
Moroccan dreams 1
Moroccan dreams 2
Battles past
Ode for the ambassador tank
Giving up, giving in
 Gaia
To run with the wind
 Left unanswered
 A bottle of wine to share with myself
 Half past October
The faerie and the voice
 A faerie storie
The storie of Faerie Glade
Nightmare on Church Street
Sherlock's opium dream 1
Young man, old soldier
Just a day
Freedom
 First rule of holes
Sherlock's opium dream 2
 Witches brew, no. 2
Lottery
Seamless
When I'm happy, I whistle
Sherlock's opium dream 3
Because of your hurtful words
The best day in a child's life
Act of the soul
A poem is born
 Under my skin

Friends
The end of a poets day
Sherlock's opium dream 4
My key to me
Love, our first time
Solitary confinement of loneliness.....and comment
Love, in desperation
 Because you can
Sherlock's opium dream 5
Murtaya
The oily rag
An ocean away
 Life's house
Bridges
Wish for an umbrella
Life's dream
Two sides of a coin
Our book
Two sides of the same coin
Homeless
That's me
 A message to myself
In the realm of the unicorn
So, you think you can read my mind
Old nick's game
Why ?
 A very special day
What DO you want ?
It's my passion
Stolen energy
Nothing is impossible
 Hand in hand
In, or out ?
 Poetry in motion
My earest friend
The silly flea
 Love over the air
 Tender moment

Dissolution
The fool in the tarot deck
The "fool" 1
The fool's journey 2
Tears of the fool 3
A dream for peace
The donger
Life in a goldfish bowl
Occam's razor
I like you
The fool's fool 4
Stormchild (.......Supernature 1)
Ocean and tea
Not far
Poetry ... poetry
H'Luanah (........Supernature 2)
For Sabeel ... Painted friends filled with dreams
Look into your heart
A mistake
We laughed
You ... are a star
Supernature (........Supernature 3)
Rewind
The smile
Jamie Allen
Into summer
Of ... you
I like your way
In Confusion
Tough love, no nonsense
Spooky, but groovy !
We.....the ark.......................1
Playing the game
Well I never
Memory from school days
The space between
We.....the ark.......................2
Ever constant

You took the moon
A time to let go
Finding my reflection
We.....the ark........................3
Plastic surgery
 A little magic
My first real car
Ithaca …. Constantine Cavafy (1863-1933)
Seek And You Shall Find
  About a Poet
The very best
  Of … nature
Of … life
 Mirror, mirror on the wall
 Love life
 Of … love
 Of   .distance
 Voyagers
 Love's sweet embrace
 Home
Dreadlocks Rod, and happiness
From the crucible....................1
The poet and Arawn................2
 Ethelgorn and Cromm.............3
 Battles eve.............................4
 Battle of Arawn and Cromm.....5
 Hawk, a poet's interlude
 Knight of hope.........................1
The darkest of knights.........................2
The battle for destiny........................3
 The devil and me
 Genie in the lamp
 A new chapter
 Elidor

dreamweaver – the poems

By
Andrew Weaver and Sonja Peacock.

This work is also available as an Ebook, as are some other works,

'dreamweaver - the poems' 2009 at www.wilmots.me.uk/dreamweaver-poems.html
'The Storie of Faerie Glade' 2010 at www.wilmots.me.uk/fairieglade.html
'A Viking Epic, Part One – Viking!' 2010 at www.wilmots.me.uk/avikingepic.html

www.ingramcontent.com/pod-product-compliance
Lightning Source LLC
Chambersburg PA
CBHW080859090426
42738CB00014B/3196

* 9 7 8 1 9 0 2 7 7 8 0 6 8 *